ALGORITHMS

SOLVE A PROBLEM!

Lyrics by BLAKE HOENA

Illustrations by SR. SÁNCHEZ

Music by MARK MALLMAN

CANTATA LEARNING

WWW.CANTATALEARNING.COM

CANTATA LEARNING

Published by Cantata Learning
1710 Roe Crest Drive
North Mankato, MN 56003
www.cantatalearning.com

Library of Congress Cataloging-in-Publication Data
Names: Hoena, B. A., author. | Sánchez, Sr., 1973– illustrator. | Mallman, Mark, composer.
Title: Algorithms : solve a problem! / by Blake Hoena ; illustrated by Sr. Sánchez ; music by Mark Mallman.
Description: North Mankato, MN : Cantata Learning, [2018] | Series: Code it! | Includes lyrics and sheet music. | Includes bibliographical references.
Identifiers: LCCN 2017017518 (print) | LCCN 2017040966 (ebook) | ISBN 9781684101467 (ebook) | ISBN 9781684101306 (hardcover : alk. paper)
Subjects: LCSH: Algorithms--Juvenile literature. | Problem solving--Juvenile literature.
Classification: LCC QA9.58 (ebook) | LCC QA9.58 .H64 2018 (print) | DDC 005--dc23
LC record available at https://lccn.loc.gov/2017017518

978-1-68410-383-6 (hardcover)

Book design and art direction, Tim Palin Creative
Editorial direction, Kellie M. Hultgren
Music direction, Elizabeth Draper
Music arranged and produced by Mark Mallman

Printed in the United States of America.
0398

ACCESS THE MUSIC!

SCAN CODE WITH MOBILE APP

CANTATALEARNING.COM

TIPS TO SUPPORT LITERACY AT HOME

WHY READING AND SINGING WITH YOUR CHILD IS SO IMPORTANT

Daily reading with your child leads to increased academic achievement. Music and songs, specifically rhyming songs, are a fun and easy way to build early literacy and language development. Music skills correlate significantly with both phonological awareness and reading development. Singing helps build vocabulary and speech development. And reading and appreciating music together is a wonderful way to strengthen your relationship.

READ AND SING EVERY DAY!

TIPS FOR USING CANTATA LEARNING BOOKS AND SONGS DURING YOUR DAILY STORY TIME

1. As you sing and read, point out the different words on the page that rhyme. Suggest other words that rhyme.
2. Memorize simple rhymes such as Itsy Bitsy Spider and sing them together. This encourages comprehension skills and early literacy skills.
3. Use the questions in the back of each book to guide your singing and storytelling.
4. Read the included sheet music with your child while you listen to the song. How do the music notes correlate to the words of the song?
5. Sing along on the go and at home. Access music by scanning the QR code on each Cantata book, or by using the included CD. You can also stream or download the music for free to your computer, smartphone, or mobile device.

Devoting time to daily reading shows that you are available for your child. Together, you are building language, literacy, and listening skills.

Have fun reading and singing!

What are **algorithms**? They are step-by-step directions to help **solve** problems. Follow the steps in order, and they can tell you how to get somewhere or how to make something. Algorithms are also used in **coding**. They are the basic **instructions** for computer programs. They tell programs how to get things done.

To learn more about algorithms, turn the page and sing along.

COOKIE
recipe
INGREDIENTS
PUT IN A BOWL
MIX
STOP
PUT SMALL BALLS
PAT FLAT
OVEN
PREHEAT TO 375°F

Algorithms are directions.
They will help you get things done.

Algorithms can solve problems.
Follow them to have some fun!

GRANDPA'S
CHOCOLATE COOKIES
INGREDIENTS
PUT IN A BOWL
MIX
STOP
PUT SMALL BALLS
PAT FLAT
OVEN
PREHEAT TO 375°F

Are you hungry for some cookies?
Then you have a baking problem.

To solve it, find a **recipe**.
Recipes are algorithms!

Follow the recipe's directions
in the order that they come.

Mix and stir to solve your problem.
You're using an algorithm!

CHOCOLATE

Algorithms are directions.
They will help you get things done.

Algorithms can solve problems.
Follow them to have some fun!

Algorithms can solve many different problems.

They are rules to games and recipes to bake.

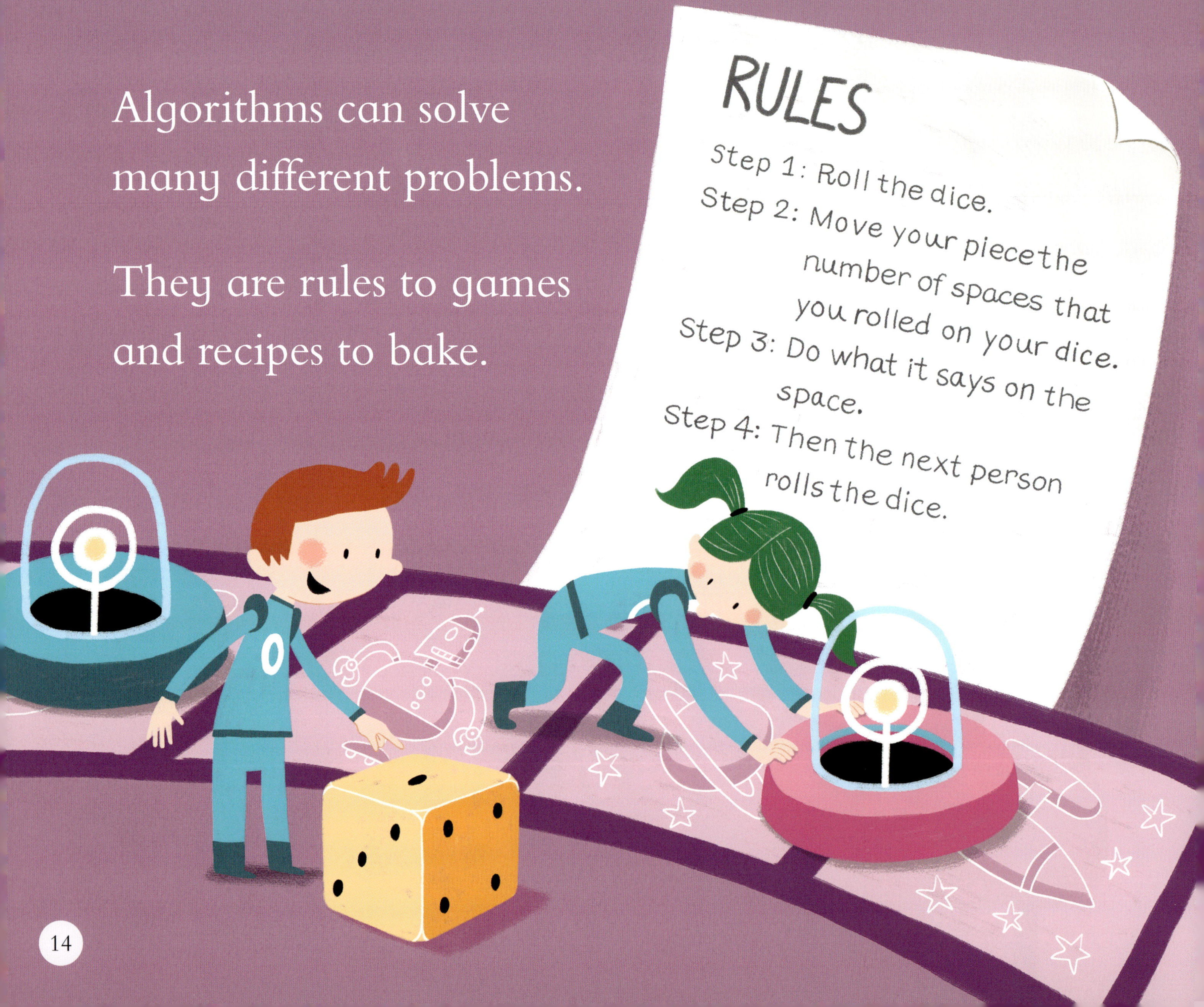

Algorithms can solve many different problems, like finding your way through a twisting maze.

Want to make a robot go?
Then you have a coding problem.

To solve it, type up some code.
You will create algorithms!

Give the robot some instructions:
how far and in what direction.

Type up code to solve your problem.
You're using an algorithm!

Algorithms are directions.
They will help you get things done.

Algorithms can solve problems.
Follow them to have some fun!

Algorithms are directions.
They will help you get things done.

Algorithms can solve problems.
Follow them to have some fun!

SONG LYRICS

Algorithms: Solve a Problem!

Algorithms are directions.
They will help you get things done.

Algorithms can solve problems.
Follow them to have some fun!

Are you hungry for some cookies?
Then you have a baking problem.

To solve it, find a recipe.
Recipes are algorithms!

Follow the recipe's directions
in the order that they come.

Mix and stir to solve your problem.
You're using an algorithm!

Algorithms are directions.
They will help you get things done.

Algorithms can solve problems.
Follow them to have some fun!

Algorithms can solve
many different problems.

They are rules to games
and recipes to bake.

Algorithms can solve
many different problems,
like finding your way
through a twisting maze.

Want to make a robot go?
Then you have a coding problem.

To solve it, type up some code.
You will create algorithms!

Give the robot some instructions:
how far and in what direction.

Type up code to solve your problem.
You're using an algorithm!

Algorithms are directions.
They will help you get things done.

Algorithms can solve problems.
Follow them to have some fun!

Algorithms are directions.
They will help you get things done.

Algorithms can solve problems.
Follow them to have some fun!

Algorithms: Solve a Problem!

Electro Pop
Mark Mallman

Chorus

Verse

Verse 2
Follow the recipe's directions
in the order that they come.
Mix and stir to solve your problem.
You're using an algorithm!

Chorus

Bridge

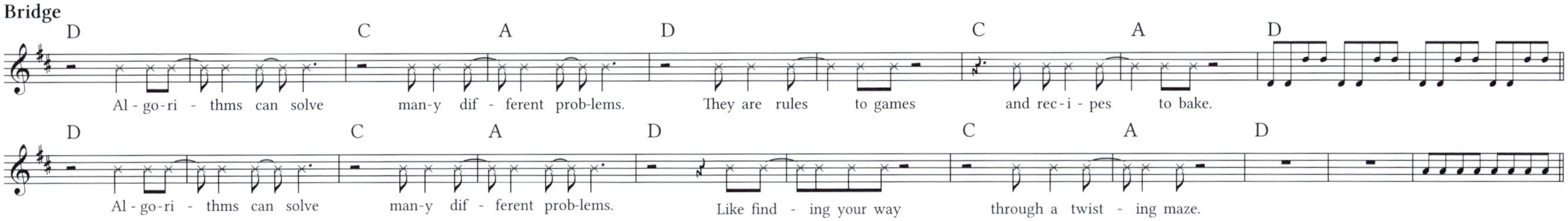

Verse 3
Want to make a robot go?
Then you have a coding problem.
To solve it, type up some code.
You will create algorithms!

Verse 4
Give the robot some instructions:
how far and in what direction.
Type up code to solve your problem.
You're using an algorithm!

Outro

GLOSSARY

algorithm—a series of steps for solving a specific problem

coding—using symbols and words to create instructions

instructions—a list of things you need to do to make something happen

recipe—a set of directions for making a food item, such as cookies

solve—to find an answer

GUIDED READING ACTIVITIES

1. This song gives you an example of an algorithm: a recipe. What other algorithms can you think of?

2. Think of something that you do almost every day. It could be getting ready for school or going to eat lunch in the cafeteria. Write down the steps to do that activity. That is an algorithm!

3. On a piece of paper, make a list of the steps you need to do to make your favorite kind of sandwich. Now cut those steps apart and mix them up. What happens if you do the steps in the wrong order? Is it still tasty?

TO LEARN MORE

Hubbard, Ben. *How Coding Works.* North Mankato, MN: Heinemann Raintree, 2017.

Higgins, Nadia. *Sequences: Order Matters!* North Mankato, MN: Cantata Learning, 2017.

Pratt, Mary K. *What Is Computer Coding?* Minneapolis: Lerner Publications, 2015.